This logbook belongs to:

_____

_____

_____

Camping life

Our travel plans and destinations

≡ Capentum

Camping life.
Our travel plans and destinations.

First edition.
Copyright © Capentum Förlag 2019

Published by Capentum Förlag, Barsebäck, Sweden.
Printed by BoD, Norderstedt, Germany, 2019
ISBN 978-91-985341-1-5

www.capentum.com

Best Campers

This is a book that over time becomes increasingly valuable based on the memories and experiences that you choose to write yourself. The value of being able to look back and re-member both routes and destinations is also a good starting point when it is time to plan for new excursions.

Here in ready-made templates you can add your own notes about dates and places, or who you were camping with or met. Route, distance, address and GPS coordinates are only part of what can be entered into the logbook. In addition, you can rate the actual location's prerequisites based on a score scale between 1-5 points, and then be able to make interest-ing comparisons with other visited places.

Our hope is now that you will have a rewarding use of this logbook on your upcoming camping trips.

Have a good camping life!

CONTENT

Area name / Place name	Date	Point	Page

CONTENT

Area name - Place name	Date	Point	Page

Destination

Location:		Campground ☐	Arrived – Departed – Year
Address:		Parking area ☐	First visit ☐ Return visit ☐
GPS:		Wild-camp ☐	Check in from / Check out until
Website:		Other ☐	Weather

Caravan ☐ Tent/Van ☐ Motorhome ☐ Cabin ☐	Site nr	Site price/day	Elec.price/day	Booked site ☐ Yes ☐ No	Price worthy ☐ Yes ☐ No

☐ **Environment (1-5)** (Location, surroundings, size of plot or cabin, maintenance, distance to electrical outlet etc.)

☐ **Sanitary (1-5)** (Standard of sanitation, room for cooking and washing, waterfilling, waste disposal etc.)

☐ **Service (1-5)** (Service from staff, info material, booking, shops, restaurants, wifi access etc.)

☐ **Activities (1-5)** (Playground, miniature golf, bath, fishing, hiking and running trails, boat/canoe/bicycle rental, etc.)

☐ Total rating (max 20p)	Child friendly ☐ Yes ☐ No	Dog friendly ☐ Yes ☐ No	For the disabled ☐ Yes ☐ No	Want to return ☐ Yes ☐ No

© Capentum Förlag

Activities

Route taken	Beginning mileage
	Ending mileage
Rest area (Place name, town, distance, standard of sanitation and surroundings etc.)	Total miles traveled
	Total travel time
	Total fuel cost

We camped with / met

Excursions / Activities

The most positive / negative with this destination

To remember before the next visit

Destination

Location:		Campground ☐	Arrived – Departed – Year

Address:		Parking area ☐	First visit ☐ Return visit ☐

GPS:		Wild-camp ☐	Check in from	Check out until

Website:		Other ☐	Weather

Caravan ☐ Tent/Van ☐ Motorhome ☐ Cabin ☐	Site nr	Site price/day	Elec.price/day	Booked site ☐ Yes ☐ No	Price worthy ☐ Yes ☐ No

☐ **Environment (1-5)** (Location, surroundings, size of plot or cabin, maintenance, distance to electrical outlet etc.)

☐ **Sanitary (1-5)** (Standard of sanitation, room for cooking and washing, waterfilling, waste disposal etc.)

☐ **Service (1-5)** (Service from staff, info material, booking, shops, restaurants, wifi access etc.)

☐ **Activities (1-5)** (Playground, miniature golf, bath, fishing, hiking and running trails, boat/canoe/bicycle rental, etc.)

☐ Total rating (max 20p)	Child friendly ☐ Yes ☐ No	Dog friendly ☐ Yes ☐ No	For the disabled ☐ Yes ☐ No	Want to return ☐ Yes ☐ No

● Capentum Förlag

Activities

| Route taken | Beginning mileage |
| | Ending mileage |

Rest area (Place name, town, distance, standard of sanitation and surroundings etc.)	Total miles traveled
	Total travel time
	Total fuel cost

We camped with / met

Excursions / Activities

The most positive / negative with this destination

To remember before the next visit

Destination

Location:		Campground ☐	Arrived – Departed – Year

Address:	Parking area ☐	First visit ☐
		Return visit ☐

GPS:	Wild-camp ☐	Check in from	Check out until

Website:	Other ☐	Weather

Caravan ☐ Tent/Van ☐	Site nr	Site price/day	Elec.price/day	Booked site	Price worthy
Motorhome ☐ Cabin ☐				☐ Yes ☐ No	☐ Yes ☐ No

☐ **Environment (1-5)** (Location, surroundings, size of plot or cabin, maintenance, distance to electrical outlet etc.)

☐ **Sanitary (1-5)** (Standard of sanitation, room for cooking and washing, waterfilling, waste disposal etc.)

☐ **Service (1-5)** (Service from staff, info material, booking, shops, restaurants, wifi access etc.)

☐ **Activities (1-5)** (Playground, miniature golf, bath, fishing, hiking and running trails, boat/canoe/bicycle rental, etc.)

☐ Total rating (max 20p)	Child friendly ☐ Yes ☐ No	Dog friendly ☐ Yes ☐ No	For the disabled ☐ Yes ☐ No	Want to return ☐ Yes ☐ No

© Capentum Förlag

Activities

Route taken	Beginning mileage
	Ending mileage
Rest area (Place name, town, distance, standard of sanitation and surroundings etc.)	Total miles traveled
	Total travel time
	Total fuel cost

We camped with / met

Excursions / Activities

The most positive / negative with this destination

To remember before the next visit

Destination

Location:		Campground ☐	Arrived – Departed – Year
Address:		Parking area ☐	First visit ☐ Return visit ☐
GPS:		Wild-camp ☐	Check in from / Check out until
Website:		Other ☐	Weather

Caravan ☐ Tent/Van ☐ Motorhome ☐ Cabin ☐	Site nr	Site price/day	Elec.price/day	Booked site ☐ Yes ☐ No	Price worthy ☐ Yes ☐ No

☐ **Environment (1-5)** (Location, surroundings, size of plot or cabin, maintenance, distance to electrical outlet etc.)

☐ **Sanitary (1-5)** (Standard of sanitation, room for cooking and washing, waterfilling, waste disposal etc.)

☐ **Service (1-5)** (Service from staff, info material, booking, shops, restaurants, wifi access etc.)

☐ **Activities (1-5)** (Playground, miniature golf, bath, fishing, hiking and running trails, boat/canoe/bicycle rental, etc.)

☐ Total rating (max 20p)	Child friendly ☐ Yes ☐ No	Dog friendly ☐ Yes ☐ No	For the disabled ☐ Yes ☐ No	Want to return ☐ Yes ☐ No

© Capentum Förlag

Activities

Route taken	Beginning mileage
	Ending mileage

Rest area (Place name, town, distance, standard of sanitation and surroundings etc.)	Total miles traveled
	Total travel time
	Total fuel cost

We camped with / met

Excursions / Activities

The most positive / negative with this destination

To remember before the next visit

Destination

Location:		Campground ☐	Arrived – Departed – Year

Address:		Parking area ☐	First visit ☐ Return visit ☐

GPS:		Wild-camp ☐	Check in from	Check out until

Website:		Other ☐	Weather

Caravan ☐ Tent/Van ☐ Motorhome ☐ Cabin ☐	Site nr	Site price/day	Elec.price/day	Booked site ☐ Yes ☐ No	Price worthy ☐ Yes ☐ No

☐ **Environment (1-5)** (Location, surroundings, size of plot or cabin, maintenance, distance to electrical outlet etc.)

☐ **Sanitary (1-5)** (Standard of sanitation, room for cooking and washing, waterfilling, waste disposal etc.)

☐ **Service (1-5)** (Service from staff, info material, booking, shops, restaurants, wifi access etc.)

☐ **Activities (1-5)** (Playground, miniature golf, bath, fishing, hiking and running trails, boat/canoe/bicycle rental, etc.)

☐ Total rating (max 20p)	Child friendly ☐ Yes ☐ No	Dog friendly ☐ Yes ☐ No	For the disabled ☐ Yes ☐ No	Want to return ☐ Yes ☐ No

Activities

Route taken		Beginning mileage
		Ending mileage
Rest area (Place name, town, distance, standard of sanitation and surroundings etc.)		Total miles traveled
		Total travel time
		Total fuel cost

We camped with / met

Excursions / Activities

The most positive / negative with this destination

To remember before the next visit

Destination

Location:		Campground ☐	Arrived – Departed – Year	
Address:		Parking area ☐	First visit ☐ Return visit ☐	
GPS:		Wild-camp ☐	Check in from	Check out until
Website:		Other ☐	Weather	

Caravan ☐ Motorhome ☐	Tent/Van ☐ Cabin ☐	Site nr	Site price/day	Elec.price/day	Booked site ☐ Yes ☐ No	Price worthy ☐ Yes ☐ No

☐ **Environment (1-5)** (Location, surroundings, size of plot or cabin, maintenance, distance to electrical outlet etc.)

☐ **Sanitary (1-5)** (Standard of sanitation, room for cooking and washing, waterfilling, waste disposal etc.)

☐ **Service (1-5)** (Service from staff, info material, booking, shops, restaurants, wifi access etc.)

☐ **Activities (1-5)** (Playground, miniature golf, bath, fishing, hiking and running trails, boat/canoe/bicycle rental, etc.)

☐ Total rating (max 20p)	Child friendly ☐ Yes ☐ No	Dog friendly ☐ Yes ☐ No	For the disabled ☐ Yes ☐ No	Want to return ☐ Yes ☐ No

Capentum Förlag

Activities

	Beginning mileage
Route taken	
	Ending mileage
Rest area (Place name, town, distance, standard of sanitation and surroundings etc.)	Total miles traveled
	Total travel time
	Total fuel cost

We camped with / met

Excursions / Activities

The most positive / negative with this destination

To remember before the next visit

Destination				

	Campground ☐	Arrived – Departed – Year
Location:		
Address:	Parking area ☐	First visit ☐ Return visit ☐
GPS:	Wild-camp ☐	Check in from / Check out until
Website:	Other ☐	Weather

Caravan ☐ Tent/Van ☐ Motorhome ☐ Cabin ☐	Site nr	Site price/day	Elec.price/day	Booked site ☐ Yes ☐ No	Price worthy ☐ Yes ☐ No

☐ **Environment (1-5)** (Location, surroundings, size of plot or cabin, maintenance, distance to electrical outlet etc.)

☐ **Sanitary (1-5)** (Standard of sanitation, room for cooking and washing, waterfilling, waste disposal etc.)

☐ **Service (1-5)** (Service from staff, info material, booking, shops, restaurants, wifi access etc.)

☐ **Activities (1-5)** (Playground, miniature golf, bath, fishing, hiking and running trails, boat/canoe/bicycle rental, etc.)

☐ Total rating (max 20p)	Child friendly ☐ Yes ☐ No	Dog friendly ☐ Yes ☐ No	For the disabled ☐ Yes ☐ No	Want to return ☐ Yes ☐ No

© Capentum Förlag

Activities

Route taken	Beginning mileage
	Ending mileage
Rest area (Place name, town, distance, standard of sanitation and surroundings etc.)	Total miles traveled
	Total travel time
	Total fuel cost

We camped with / met

Excursions / Activities

The most positive / negative with this destination

To remember before the next visit

Destination

Location:		Campground ☐	Arrived – Departed – Year
Address:		Parking area ☐	First visit ☐ Return visit ☐
GPS:		Wild-camp ☐	Check in from / Check out until
Website:		Other ☐	Weather

Caravan ☐ Motorhome ☐	Tent/Van ☐ Cabin ☐	Site nr	Site price/day	Elec.price/day	Booked site ☐ Yes ☐ No	Price worthy ☐ Yes ☐ No

☐ **Environment (1-5)** (Location, surroundings, size of plot or cabin, maintenance, distance to electrical outlet etc.)

☐ **Sanitary (1-5)** (Standard of sanitation, room for cooking and washing, waterfilling, waste disposal etc.)

☐ **Service (1-5)** (Service from staff, info material, booking, shops, restaurants, wifi access etc.)

☐ **Activities (1-5)** (Playground, miniature golf, bath, fishing, hiking and running trails, boat/canoe/bicycle rental, etc.)

☐ Total rating (max 20p)	Child friendly ☐ Yes ☐ No	Dog friendly ☐ Yes ☐ No	For the disabled ☐ Yes ☐ No	Want to return ☐ Yes ☐ No

© Capentum Förlag

Activities

Route taken		Beginning mileage
		Ending mileage
Rest area (Place name, town, distance, standard of sanitation and surroundings etc.)		Total miles traveled
		Total travel time
		Total fuel cost

We camped with / met

Excursions / Activities

The most positive / negative with this destination

To remember before the next visit

Destination

Location:		Campground ☐	Arrived - Departed - Year
Address:		Parking area ☐	First visit ☐ Return visit ☐
GPS:		Wild-camp ☐	Check in from / Check out until
Website:		Other ☐	Weather

Caravan ☐ Motorhome ☐	Tent/Van ☐ Cabin ☐	Site nr	Site price/day	Elec.price/day	Booked site ☐Yes ☐No	Price worthy ☐Yes ☐No

☐ **Environment (1-5)** (Location, surroundings, size of plot or cabin, maintenance, distance to electrical outlet etc.)

☐ **Sanitary (1-5)** (Standard of sanitation, room for cooking and washing, waterfilling, waste disposal etc.)

☐ **Service (1-5)** (Service from staff, info material, booking, shops, restaurants, wifi access etc.)

☐ **Activities (1-5)** (Playground, miniature golf, bath, fishing, hiking and running trails, boat/canoe/bicycle rental, etc.)

☐ Total rating (max 20p)	Child friendly ☐Yes ☐No	Dog friendly ☐Yes ☐No	For the disabled ☐Yes ☐No	Want to return ☐Yes ☐No

Activities

Route taken	Beginning mileage
	Ending mileage

Rest area (Place name, town, distance, standard of sanitation and surroundings etc.)	Total miles traveled
	Total travel time
	Total fuel cost

We camped with / met

Excursions / Activities

The most positive / negative with this destination

To remember before the next visit

Destination

Location:		Campground ☐	Arrived – Departed – Year
Address:		Parking area ☐	First visit ☐ Return visit ☐
GPS:		Wild-camp ☐	Check in from	Check out until
Website:		Other ☐	Weather

Caravan ☐ Tent/Van ☐ Motorhome ☐ Cabin ☐	Site nr	Site price/day	Elec.price/day	Booked site ☐ Yes ☐ No	Price worthy ☐ Yes ☐ No

☐ **Environment (1-5)** (Location, surroundings, size of plot or cabin, maintenance, distance to electrical outlet etc.)

☐ **Sanitary (1-5)** (Standard of sanitation, room for cooking and washing, waterfilling, waste disposal etc.)

☐ **Service (1-5)** (Service from staff, info material, booking, shops, restaurants, wifi access etc.)

☐ **Activities (1-5)** (Playground, miniature golf, bath, fishing, hiking and running trails, boat/canoe/bicycle rental, etc.)

☐ Total rating (max 20p)	Child friendly ☐ Yes ☐ No	Dog friendly ☐ Yes ☐ No	For the disabled ☐ Yes ☐ No	Want to return ☐ Yes ☐ No

© Capentum Förlag

Activities

Route taken	Beginning mileage
	Ending mileage
Rest area (Place name, town, distance, standard of sanitation and surroundings etc.)	Total miles traveled
	Total travel time
	Total fuel cost

We camped with / met

Excursions / Activities

The most positive / negative with this destination

To remember before the next visit

Destination

Location:	Campground ☐	Arrived – Departed – Year	
Address:	Parking area ☐	First visit ☐	
		Return visit ☐	
GPS:	Wild-camp ☐	Check in from	Check out until
Website:	Other ☐	Weather	

Caravan ☐ Motorhome ☐	Tent/Van ☐ Cabin ☐	Site nr	Site price/day	Elec.price/day	Booked site ☐ Yes ☐ No	Price worthy ☐ Yes ☐ No

☐ **Environment (1-5)**   (Location, surroundings, size of plot or cabin, maintenance, distance to electrical outlet etc.)

☐ **Sanitary (1-5)**   (Standard of sanitation, room for cooking and washing, waterfilling, waste disposal etc.)

☐ **Service (1-5)**   (Service from staff, info material, booking, shops, restaurants, wifi access etc.)

☐ **Activities (1-5)**   (Playground, miniature golf, bath, fishing, hiking and running trails, boat/canoe/bicycle rental, etc.)

☐ Total rating (max 20p)	Child friendly ☐ Yes ☐ No	Dog friendly ☐ Yes ☐ No	For the disabled ☐ Yes ☐ No	Want to return ☐ Yes ☐ No

◉ Capentum Förlag

Activities

Route taken	Beginning mileage
	Ending mileage

Rest area (Place name, town, distance, standard of sanitation and surroundings etc.)	Total miles traveled
	Total travel time
	Total fuel cost

We camped with / met

Excursions / Activities

The most positive / negative with this destination

To remember before the next visit

Destination

Location:		Campground ☐	Arrived – Departed – Year
Address:		Parking area ☐	First visit ☐ Return visit ☐
GPS:		Wild-camp ☐	Check in from / Check out until
Website:		Other ☐	Weather

Caravan ☐ Tent/Van ☐ Motorhome ☐ Cabin ☐	Site nr	Site price/day	Elec.price/day	Booked site ☐ Yes ☐ No	Price worthy ☐ Yes ☐ No

☐ **Environment (1-5)** (Location, surroundings, size of plot or cabin, maintenance, distance to electrical outlet etc.)

☐ **Sanitary (1-5)** (Standard of sanitation, room for cooking and washing, waterfilling, waste disposal etc.)

☐ **Service (1-5)** (Service from staff, info material, booking, shops, restaurants, wifi access etc.)

☐ **Activities (1-5)** (Playground, miniature golf, bath, fishing, hiking and running trails, boat/canoe/bicycle rental, etc.)

☐ Total rating (max 20p)	Child friendly ☐ Yes ☐ No	Dog friendly ☐ Yes ☐ No	For the disabled ☐ Yes ☐ No	Want to return ☐ Yes ☐ No

© Capentum Förlag

Activities

Route taken	Beginning mileage
	Ending mileage
Rest area (Place name, town, distance, standard of sanitation and surroundings etc.)	Total miles traveled
	Total travel time
	Total fuel cost

We camped with / met

Excursions / Activities

The most positive / negative with this destination

To remember before the next visit

Destination

Location:	Campground ☐	Arrived – Departed – Year
Address:	Parking area ☐	First visit ☐ Return visit ☐
GPS:	Wild-camp ☐	Check in from / Check out until
Website:	Other ☐	Weather

Caravan ☐ Motorhome ☐	Tent/Van ☐ Cabin ☐	Site nr	Site price/day	Elec.price/day	Booked site ☐ Yes ☐ No	Price worthy ☐ Yes ☐ No

☐ **Environment** (1-5) (Location, surroundings, size of plot or cabin, maintenance, distance to electrical outlet etc.)

☐ **Sanitary** (1-5) (Standard of sanitation, room for cooking and washing, waterfilling, waste disposal etc.)

☐ **Service** (1-5) (Service from staff, info material, booking, shops, restaurants, wifi access etc.)

☐ **Activities** (1-5) (Playground, miniature golf, bath, fishing, hiking and running trails, boat/canoe/bicycle rental, etc.)

☐ Total rating (max 20p)	Child friendly ☐ Yes ☐ No	Dog friendly ☐ Yes ☐ No	For the disabled ☐ Yes ☐ No	Want to return ☐ Yes ☐ No

© Capentum Förlag

Activities

Route taken	Beginning mileage
	Ending mileage

Rest area (Place name, town, distance, standard of sanitation and surroundings etc.)	Total miles traveled
	Total travel time
	Total fuel cost

We camped with / met

Excursions / Activities

The most positive / negative with this destination

To remember before the next visit

Destination

Location:		Campground ☐	Arrived – Departed – Year
Address:		Parking area ☐	First visit ☐ Return visit ☐
GPS:		Wild-camp ☐	Check in from / Check out until
Website:		Other ☐	Weather

Caravan ☐ Tent/Van ☐ Motorhome ☐ Cabin ☐	Site nr	Site price/day	Elec.price/day	Booked site ☐ Yes ☐ No	Price worthy ☐ Yes ☐ No

☐ **Environment (1-5)** (Location, surroundings, size of plot or cabin, maintenance, distance to electrical outlet etc.)

☐ **Sanitary (1-5)** (Standard of sanitation, room for cooking and washing, waterfilling, waste disposal etc.)

☐ **Service (1-5)** (Service from staff, info material, booking, shops, restaurants, wifi access etc.)

☐ **Activities (1-5)** (Playground, miniature golf, bath, fishing, hiking and running trails, boat/canoe/bicycle rental, etc.)

☐ Total rating (max 20p)	Child friendly ☐ Yes ☐ No	Dog friendly ☐ Yes ☐ No	For the disabled ☐ Yes ☐ No	Want to return ☐ Yes ☐ No

Capentum Förlag

Activities

Route taken	Beginning mileage
	Ending mileage
Rest area (Place name, town, distance, standard of sanitation and surroundings etc.)	Total miles traveled
	Total travel time
	Total fuel cost

We camped with / met

Excursions / Activities

The most positive / negative with this destination

To remember before the next visit

Destination

Location:	Campground ☐	Arrived – Departed – Year

Address: | Parking area ☐ | First visit ☐
Return visit ☐

GPS: | Wild-camp ☐ | Check in from | Check out until

Website: | Other ☐ | Weather

Caravan ☐ Tent/Van ☐	Site nr	Site price/day	Elec.price/day	Booked site ☐ Yes ☐ No	Price worthy ☐ Yes ☐ No
Motorhome ☐ Cabin ☐					

☐ **Environment (1-5)**   (Location, surroundings, size of plot or cabin, maintenance, distance to electrical outlet etc.)

☐ **Sanitary (1-5)**   (Standard of sanitation, room for cooking and washing, waterfilling, waste disposal etc.)

☐ **Service (1-5)**   (Service from staff, info material, booking, shops, restaurants, wifi access etc.)

☐ **Activities (1-5)**   (Playground, miniature golf, bath, fishing, hiking and running trails, boat/canoe/bicycle rental, etc.)

☐ Total rating (max 20p)	Child friendly ☐ Yes ☐ No	Dog friendly ☐ Yes ☐ No	For the disabled ☐ Yes ☐ No	Want to return ☐ Yes ☐ No

Activities

Route taken	Beginning mileage
	Ending mileage
Rest area (Place name, town, distance, standard of sanitation and surroundings etc.)	Total miles traveled
	Total travel time
	Total fuel cost

We camped with / met

Excursions / Activities

The most positive / negative with this destination

To remember before the next visit

Destination

Location:		Campground ☐	Arrived – Departed – Year

Address:		Parking area ☐	First visit ☐
			Return visit ☐

GPS:		Wild-camp ☐	Check in from	Check out until

Website:		Other ☐	Weather

Caravan ☐ Tent/Van ☐	Site nr	Site price/day	Elec.price/day	Booked site	Price worthy
Motorhome ☐ Cabin ☐				☐ Yes ☐ No	☐ Yes ☐ No

☐ **Environment (1-5)** (Location, surroundings, size of plot or cabin, maintenance, distance to electrical outlet etc.)

☐ **Sanitary (1-5)** (Standard of sanitation, room for cooking and washing, waterfilling, waste disposal etc.)

☐ **Service (1-5)** (Service from staff, info material, booking, shops, restaurants, wifi access etc.)

☐ **Activities (1-5)** (Playground, miniature golf, bath, fishing, hiking and running trails, boat/canoe/bicycle rental, etc.)

☐ Total rating (max 20p)	Child friendly ☐ Yes ☐ No	Dog friendly ☐ Yes ☐ No	For the disabled ☐ Yes ☐ No	Want to return ☐ Yes ☐ No

Activities

Route taken	Beginning mileage
	Ending mileage
Rest area (Place name, town, distance, standard of sanitation and surroundings etc.)	Total miles traveled
	Total travel time
	Total fuel cost

We camped with / met

Excursions / Activities

The most positive / negative with this destination

To remember before the next visit

Destination

Location:		Campground ☐	Arrived – Departed – Year
Address:		Parking area ☐	First visit ☐ Return visit ☐
GPS:		Wild-camp ☐	Check in from / Check out until
Website:		Other ☐	Weather

Caravan ☐ Tent/Van ☐ Motorhome ☐ Cabin ☐	Site nr	Site price/day	Elec.price/day	Booked site ☐Yes ☐No	Price worthy ☐Yes ☐No

☐ **Environment (1-5)** (Location, surroundings, size of plot or cabin, maintenance, distance to electrical outlet etc.)

☐ **Sanitary (1-5)** (Standard of sanitation, room for cooking and washing, waterfilling, waste disposal etc.)

☐ **Service (1-5)** (Service from staff, info material, booking, shops, restaurants, wifi access etc.)

☐ **Activities (1-5)** (Playground, miniature golf, bath, fishing, hiking and running trails, boat/canoe/bicycle rental, etc.)

☐ Total rating (max 20p)	Child friendly ☐Yes ☐No	Dog friendly ☐Yes ☐No	For the disabled ☐Yes ☐No	Want to return ☐Yes ☐No

Activities

Route taken	Beginning mileage
	Ending mileage

Rest area (Place name, town, distance, standard of sanitation and surroundings etc.)	Total miles traveled
	Total travel time
	Total fuel cost

We camped with / met

Excursions / Activities

The most positive / negative with this destination

To remember before the next visit

Destination

Location:	Campground ☐	Arrived – Departed – Year
Address:	Parking area ☐	First visit ☐ Return visit ☐
GPS:	Wild-camp ☐	Check in from / Check out until
Website:	Other ☐	Weather

| Caravan ☐ Tent/Van ☐
 Motorhome ☐ Cabin ☐ | Site nr | Site price/day | Elec.price/day | Booked site
 ☐ Yes ☐ No | Price worthy
 ☐ Yes ☐ No |

☐ **Environment (1-5)** (Location, surroundings, size of plot or cabin, maintenance, distance to electrical outlet etc.)

☐ **Sanitary (1-5)** (Standard of sanitation, room for cooking and washing, waterfilling, waste disposal etc.)

☐ **Service (1-5)** (Service from staff, info material, booking, shops, restaurants, wifi access etc.)

☐ **Activities (1-5)** (Playground, miniature golf, bath, fishing, hiking and running trails, boat/canoe/bicycle rental, etc.)

| ☐ Total rating (max 20p) | Child friendly
 ☐ Yes ☐ No | Dog friendly
 ☐ Yes ☐ No | For the disabled
 ☐ Yes ☐ No | Want to return
 ☐ Yes ☐ No |

© Capentum Förlag

Activities

Route taken	Beginning mileage
	Ending mileage
Rest area (Place name, town, distance, standard of sanitation and surroundings etc.)	Total miles traveled
	Total travel time
	Total fuel cost

We camped with / met

Excursions / Activities

The most positive / negative with this destination

To remember before the next visit

Destination

Location:		Campground ☐	Arrived – Departed – Year	
Address:		Parking area ☐	First visit ☐ Return visit ☐	
GPS:		Wild-camp ☐	Check in from	Check out until
Website:		Other ☐	Weather	

Caravan ☐ Tent/Van ☐ Motorhome ☐ Cabin ☐	Site nr	Site price/day	Elec.price/day	Booked site ☐ Yes ☐ No	Price worthy ☐ Yes ☐ No

☐ **Environment (1-5)** (Location, surroundings, size of plot or cabin, maintenance, distance to electrical outlet etc.)

☐ **Sanitary (1-5)** (Standard of sanitation, room for cooking and washing, waterfilling, waste disposal etc.)

☐ **Service (1-5)** (Service from staff, info material, booking, shops, restaurants, wifi access etc.)

☐ **Activities (1-5)** (Playground, miniature golf, bath, fishing, hiking and running trails, boat/canoe/bicycle rental, etc.)

☐ Total rating (max 20p)	Child friendly ☐ Yes ☐ No	Dog friendly ☐ Yes ☐ No	For the disabled ☐ Yes ☐ No	Want to return ☐ Yes ☐ No

© Capentum Förlag

Activities

Route taken	Beginning mileage
	Ending mileage
Rest area (Place name, town, distance, standard of sanitation and surroundings etc.)	Total miles traveled
	Total travel time
	Total fuel cost

We camped with / met

Excursions / Activities

The most positive / negative with this destination

To remember before the next visit

Destination

Location:		Campground ☐	Arrived – Departed – Year
Address:		Parking area ☐	First visit ☐ Return visit ☐
GPS:		Wild-camp ☐	Check in from / Check out until
Website:		Other ☐	Weather

Caravan ☐ Tent/Van ☐ Motorhome ☐ Cabin ☐	Site nr	Site price/day	Elec.price/day	Booked site ☐ Yes ☐ No	Price worthy ☐ Yes ☐ No

☐ **Environment (1-5)** (Location, surroundings, size of plot or cabin, maintenance, distance to electrical outlet etc.)

☐ **Sanitary (1-5)** (Standard of sanitation, room for cooking and washing, waterfilling, waste disposal etc.)

☐ **Service (1-5)** (Service from staff, info material, booking, shops, restaurants, wifi access etc.)

☐ **Activities (1-5)** (Playground, miniature golf, bath, fishing, hiking and running trails, boat/canoe/bicycle rental, etc.)

☐ Total rating (max 20p)	Child friendly ☐ Yes ☐ No	Dog friendly ☐ Yes ☐ No	For the disabled ☐ Yes ☐ No	Want to return ☐ Yes ☐ No

© Capentum Förlag

Activities

Route taken	Beginning mileage
	Ending mileage

Rest area (Place name, town, distance, standard of sanitation and surroundings etc.)	Total miles traveled
	Total travel time
	Total fuel cost

We camped with / met

Excursions / Activities

The most positive / negative with this destination

To remember before the next visit

Destination

Location:	Campground ☐	Arrived - Departed - Year

Address:	Parking area ☐	First visit ☐
		Return visit ☐

GPS:	Wild-camp ☐	Check in from	Check out until

Website:	Other ☐	Weather

Caravan ☐ Tent/Van ☐	Site nr	Site price/day	Elec.price/day	Booked site	Price worthy
Motorhome ☐ Cabin ☐				☐ Yes ☐ No	☐ Yes ☐ No

☐ **Environment (1-5)**   (Location, surroundings, size of plot or cabin, maintenance, distance to electrical outlet etc.)

☐ **Sanitary (1-5)**   (Standard of sanitation, room for cooking and washing, waterfilling, waste disposal etc.)

☐ **Service (1-5)**   (Service from staff, info material, booking, shops, restaurants, wifi access etc.)

☐ **Activities (1-5)**   (Playground, miniature golf, bath, fishing, hiking and running trails, boat/canoe/bicycle rental, etc.)

☐ Total rating (max 20p)	Child friendly	Dog friendly	For the disabled	Want to return
	☐ Yes ☐ No	☐ Yes ☐ No	☐ Yes ☐ No	☐ Yes ☐ No

© Capentum Förlag

Activities

Route taken		Beginning mileage
		Ending mileage
Rest area (Place name, town, distance, standard of sanitation and surroundings etc.)		Total miles traveled
		Total travel time
		Total fuel cost

We camped with / met

Excursions / Activities

The most positive / negative with this destination

To remember before the next visit

Destination

Location:	Campground ☐	Arrived – Departed – Year
Address:	Parking area ☐	First visit ☐ Return visit ☐
GPS:	Wild-camp ☐	Check in from / Check out until
Website:	Other ☐	Weather

Caravan ☐ Tent/Van ☐ Motorhome ☐ Cabin ☐	Site nr	Site price/day	Elec.price/day	Booked site ☐ Yes ☐ No	Price worthy ☐ Yes ☐ No

☐ **Environment (1-5)** (Location, surroundings, size of plot or cabin, maintenance, distance to electrical outlet etc.)

☐ **Sanitary (1-5)** (Standard of sanitation, room for cooking and washing, waterfilling, waste disposal etc.)

☐ **Service (1-5)** (Service from staff, info material, booking, shops, restaurants, wifi access etc.)

☐ **Activities (1-5)** (Playground, miniature golf, bath, fishing, hiking and running trails, boat/canoe/bicycle rental, etc.)

☐ Total rating (max 20p)	Child friendly ☐ Yes ☐ No	Dog friendly ☐ Yes ☐ No	For the disabled ☐ Yes ☐ No	Want to return ☐ Yes ☐ No

© Capentum Förlag

Activities

| Route taken | Beginning mileage |
| | Ending mileage |

Rest area (Place name, town, distance, standard of sanitation and surroundings etc.)

| Total miles traveled |
| Total travel time |
| Total fuel cost |

We camped with / met

Excursions / Activities

The most positive / negative with this destination

To remember before the next visit

Destination

Location:	Campground ☐	Arrived – Departed – Year

Address:	Parking area ☐	First visit ☐ Return visit ☐

GPS:	Wild-camp ☐	Check in from	Check out until

Website:	Other ☐	Weather

Caravan ☐ Tent/Van ☐ Motorhome ☐ Cabin ☐	Site nr	Site price/day	Elec.price/day	Booked site ☐ Yes ☐ No	Price worthy ☐ Yes ☐ No

☐ **Environment** (1-5) (Location, surroundings, size of plot or cabin, maintenance, distance to electrical outlet etc.)

☐ **Sanitary** (1-5) (Standard of sanitation, room for cooking and washing, waterfilling, waste disposal etc.)

☐ **Service** (1-5) (Service from staff, info material, booking, shops, restaurants, wifi access etc.)

☐ **Activities** (1-5) (Playground, miniature golf, bath, fishing, hiking and running trails, boat/canoe/bicycle rental, etc.)

☐ Total rating (max 20p)	Child friendly ☐ Yes ☐ No	Dog friendly ☐ Yes ☐ No	For the disabled ☐ Yes ☐ No	Want to return ☐ Yes ☐ No

● Capentum Förlag

Activities

Route taken	Beginning mileage
	Ending mileage

Rest area (Place name, town, distance, standard of sanitation and surroundings etc.)	Total miles traveled
	Total travel time
	Total fuel cost

We camped with / met

Excursions / Activities

The most positive / negative with this destination

To remember before the next visit

Destination

Location:		Campground ☐	Arrived – Departed – Year
Address:		Parking area ☐	First visit ☐ Return visit ☐
GPS:		Wild-camp ☐	Check in from / Check out until
Website:		Other ☐	Weather

Caravan ☐ Motorhome ☐	Tent/Van ☐ Cabin ☐	Site nr	Site price/day	Elec.price/day	Booked site ☐ Yes ☐ No	Price worthy ☐ Yes ☐ No

☐ Environment (1-5) (Location, surroundings, size of plot or cabin, maintenance, distance to electrical outlet etc.)

☐ Sanitary (1-5) (Standard of sanitation, room for cooking and washing, waterfilling, waste disposal etc.)

☐ Service (1-5) (Service from staff, info material, booking, shops, restaurants, wifi access etc.)

☐ Activities (1-5) (Playground, miniature golf, bath, fishing, hiking and running trails, boat/canoe/bicycle rental, etc.)

☐ Total rating (max 20p)	Child friendly ☐ Yes ☐ No	Dog friendly ☐ Yes ☐ No	For the disabled ☐ Yes ☐ No	Want to return ☐ Yes ☐ No

☉ Capentum Förlag

Activities

Route taken	Beginning mileage
	Ending mileage
Rest area (Place name, town, distance, standard of sanitation and surroundings etc.)	Total miles traveled
	Total travel time
	Total fuel cost

We camped with / met

Excursions / Activities

The most positive / negative with this destination

To remember before the next visit

Destination

Location:	Campground ☐	Arrived - Departed - Year

Address:	Parking area ☐	First visit ☐
		Return visit ☐

GPS:	Wild-camp ☐	Check in from	Check out until

Website:	Other ☐	Weather

Caravan ☐ Tent/Van ☐	Site nr	Site price/day	Elec.price/day	Booked site	Price worthy
Motorhome ☐ Cabin ☐				☐Yes ☐No	☐Yes ☐No

☐ **Environment (1-5)**   (Location, surroundings, size of plot or cabin, maintenance, distance to electrical outlet etc.)

☐ **Sanitary (1-5)**   (Standard of sanitation, room for cooking and washing, waterfilling, waste disposal etc.)

☐ **Service (1-5)**   (Service from staff, info material, booking, shops, restaurants, wifi access etc.)

☐ **Activities (1-5)**   (Playground, miniature golf, bath, fishing, hiking and running trails, boat/canoe/bicycle rental, etc.)

☐ Total rating (max 20p)	Child friendly ☐Yes ☐No	Dog friendly ☐Yes ☐No	For the disabled ☐Yes ☐No	Want to return ☐Yes ☐No

Activities

Route taken	Beginning mileage
	Ending mileage
Rest area (Place name, town, distance, standard of sanitation and surroundings etc.)	Total miles traveled
	Total travel time
	Total fuel cost

We camped with / met

Excursions / Activities

The most positive / negative with this destination

To remember before the next visit

Destination

Location:	Campground ☐	Arrived – Departed – Year	
Address:	Parking area ☐	First visit ☐ Return visit ☐	
GPS:	Wild-camp ☐	Check in from	Check out until
Website:	Other ☐	Weather	

Caravan ☐ Tent/Van ☐ Motorhome ☐ Cabin ☐	Site nr	Site price/day	Elec.price/day	Booked site ☐ Yes ☐ No	Price worthy ☐ Yes ☐ No

☐ **Environment (1-5)** (Location, surroundings, size of plot or cabin, maintenance, distance to electrical outlet etc.)

☐ **Sanitary (1-5)** (Standard of sanitation, room for cooking and washing, waterfilling, waste disposal etc.)

☐ **Service (1-5)** (Service from staff, info material, booking, shops, restaurants, wifi access etc.)

☐ **Activities (1-5)** (Playground, miniature golf, bath, fishing, hiking and running trails, boat/canoe/bicycle rental, etc.)

☐ Total rating (max 20p)	Child friendly ☐ Yes ☐ No	Dog friendly ☐ Yes ☐ No	For the disabled ☐ Yes ☐ No	Want to return ☐ Yes ☐ No

☉ Capentum Förlag

Activities

Route taken		Beginning mileage
		Ending mileage
Rest area (Place name, town, distance, standard of sanitation and surroundings etc.)		Total miles traveled
		Total travel time
		Total fuel cost

We camped with / met

Excursions / Activities

The most positive / negative with this destination

To remember before the next visit

Destination

Location:		Campground ☐	Arrived – Departed – Year
Address:		Parking area ☐	First visit ☐ Return visit ☐
GPS:		Wild-camp ☐	Check in from / Check out until
Website:		Other ☐	Weather

Caravan ☐ Tent/Van ☐ Motorhome ☐ Cabin ☐	Site nr	Site price/day	Elec.price/day	Booked site ☐Yes ☐No	Price worthy ☐Yes ☐No

☐ **Environment (1-5)** (Location, surroundings, size of plot or cabin, maintenance, distance to electrical outlet etc.)

☐ **Sanitary (1-5)** (Standard of sanitation, room for cooking and washing, waterfilling, waste disposal etc.)

☐ **Service (1-5)** (Service from staff, info material, booking, shops, restaurants, wifi access etc.)

☐ **Activities (1-5)** (Playground, miniature golf, bath, fishing, hiking and running trails, boat/canoe/bicycle rental, etc.)

☐ Total rating (max 20p)	Child friendly ☐Yes ☐No	Dog friendly ☐Yes ☐No	For the disabled ☐Yes ☐No	Want to return ☐Yes ☐No

☉ Capentum Förlag

Activities

Route taken		Beginning mileage
		Ending mileage
Rest area (Place name, town, distance, standard of sanitation and surroundings etc.)		Total miles traveled
		Total travel time
		Total fuel cost

We camped with / met

Excursions / Activities

The most positive / negative with this destination

To remember before the next visit

Destination

Location:	Campground ☐	Arrived – Departed – Year
Address:	Parking area ☐	First visit ☐ Return visit ☐
GPS:	Wild-camp ☐	Check in from / Check out until
Website:	Other ☐	Weather

Caravan ☐ Tent/Van ☐ Motorhome ☐ Cabin ☐	Site nr	Site price/day	Elec.price/day	Booked site ☐ Yes ☐ No	Price worthy ☐ Yes ☐ No

☐ **Environment (1–5)** (Location, surroundings, size of plot or cabin, maintenance, distance to electrical outlet etc.)

☐ **Sanitary (1–5)** (Standard of sanitation, room for cooking and washing, waterfilling, waste disposal etc.)

☐ **Service (1–5)** (Service from staff, info material, booking, shops, restaurants, wifi access etc.)

☐ **Activities (1–5)** (Playground, miniature golf, bath, fishing, hiking and running trails, boat/canoe/bicycle rental, etc.)

☐ Total rating (max 20p)	Child friendly ☐ Yes ☐ No	Dog friendly ☐ Yes ☐ No	For the disabled ☐ Yes ☐ No	Want to return ☐ Yes ☐ No

☺ Capentum Förlag

Activities

Route taken	**Beginning mileage**
	Ending mileage
Rest area (Place name, town, distance, standard of sanitation and surroundings etc.)	**Total miles traveled**
	Total travel time
	Total fuel cost

We camped with / met

Excursions / Activities

The most positive / negative with this destination

To remember before the next visit

Destination

Location:	Campground ☐	Arrived – Departed – Year
Address:	Parking area ☐	First visit ☐ Return visit ☐
GPS:	Wild-camp ☐	Check in from	Check out until
Website:	Other ☐	Weather

Caravan ☐ Tent/Van ☐ Motorhome ☐ Cabin ☐	Site nr	Site price/day	Elec.price/day	Booked site ☐ Yes ☐ No	Price worthy ☐ Yes ☐ No

☐ **Environment (1-5)**   (Location, surroundings, size of plot or cabin, maintenance, distance to electrical outlet etc.)

☐ **Sanitary (1-5)**   (Standard of sanitation, room for cooking and washing, waterfilling, waste disposal etc.)

☐ **Service (1-5)**   (Service from staff, info material, booking, shops, restaurants, wifi access etc.)

☐ **Activities (1-5)**   (Playground, miniature golf, bath, fishing, hiking and running trails, boat/canoe/bicycle rental, etc.)

☐ Total rating (max 20p)	Child friendly ☐ Yes ☐ No	Dog friendly ☐ Yes ☐ No	For the disabled ☐ Yes ☐ No	Want to return ☐ Yes ☐ No

Activities

Route taken	Beginning mileage
	Ending mileage

Rest area (Place name, town, distance, standard of sanitation and surroundings etc.)	Total miles traveled
	Total travel time
	Total fuel cost

We camped with / met

Excursions / Activities

The most positive / negative with this destination

To remember before the next visit

Destination

Location:	Campground ☐	Arrived – Departed – Year
Address:	Parking area ☐	First visit ☐ Return visit ☐
GPS:	Wild-camp ☐	Check in from / Check out until
Website:	Other ☐	Weather

Caravan ☐ Tent/Van ☐ Motorhome ☐ Cabin ☐	Site nr	Site price/day	Elec.price/day	Booked site ☐ Yes ☐ No	Price worthy ☐ Yes ☐ No

☐ **Environment (1-5)** (Location, surroundings, size of plot or cabin, maintenance, distance to electrical outlet etc.)

☐ **Sanitary (1-5)** (Standard of sanitation, room for cooking and washing, waterfilling, waste disposal etc.)

☐ **Service (1-5)** (Service from staff, info material, booking, shops, restaurants, wifi access etc.)

☐ **Activities (1-5)** (Playground, miniature golf, bath, fishing, hiking and running trails, boat/canoe/bicycle rental, etc.)

☐ Total rating (max 20p)	Child friendly ☐ Yes ☐ No	Dog friendly ☐ Yes ☐ No	For the disabled ☐ Yes ☐ No	Want to return ☐ Yes ☐ No

⊙ Capentum Förlag

Activities

| Route taken | Beginning mileage |
| | Ending mileage |

Rest area (Place name, town, distance, standard of sanitation and surroundings etc.)	Total miles traveled
	Total travel time
	Total fuel cost

We camped with / met

Excursions / Activities

The most positive / negative with this destination

To remember before the next visit

Destination

Location:		Campground ☐	Arrived – Departed – Year	
Address:		Parking area ☐	First visit ☐ Return visit ☐	
GPS:		Wild-camp ☐	Check in from	Check out until
Website:		Other ☐	Weather	

Caravan ☐ Tent/Van ☐ Motorhome ☐ Cabin ☐	Site nr	Site price/day	Elec.price/day	Booked site ☐ Yes ☐ No	Price worthy ☐ Yes ☐ No

☐ **Environment (1-5)**   (Location, surroundings, size of plot or cabin, maintenance, distance to electrical outlet etc.)

☐ **Sanitary (1-5)**   (Standard of sanitation, room for cooking and washing, waterfilling, waste disposal etc.)

☐ **Service (1-5)**   (Service from staff, info material, booking, shops, restaurants, wifi access etc.)

☐ **Activities (1-5)**   (Playground, miniature golf, bath, fishing, hiking and running trails, boat/canoe/bicycle rental, etc.)

☐ Total rating (max 20p)	Child friendly ☐ Yes ☐ No	Dog friendly ☐ Yes ☐ No	For the disabled ☐ Yes ☐ No	Want to return ☐ Yes ☐ No

Activities

Route taken		Beginning mileage
		Ending mileage
Rest area (Place name, town, distance, standard of sanitation and surroundings etc.)		Total miles traveled
		Total travel time
		Total fuel cost

We camped with / met

Excursions / Activities

The most positive / negative with this destination

To remember before the next visit

Destination

Location:	Campground ☐	Arrived – Departed – Year
Address:	Parking area ☐	First visit ☐ Return visit ☐
GPS:	Wild-camp ☐	Check in from / Check out until
Website:	Other ☐	Weather

Caravan ☐ Tent/Van ☐ Motorhome ☐ Cabin ☐	Site nr	Site price/day	Elec.price/day	Booked site ☐ Yes ☐ No	Price worthy ☐ Yes ☐ No

☐ **Environment (1-5)** (Location, surroundings, size of plot or cabin, maintenance, distance to electrical outlet etc.)

☐ **Sanitary (1-5)** (Standard of sanitation, room for cooking and washing, waterfilling, waste disposal etc.)

☐ **Service (1-5)** (Service from staff, info material, booking, shops, restaurants, wifi access etc.)

☐ **Activities (1-5)** (Playground, miniature golf, bath, fishing, hiking and running trails, boat/canoe/bicycle rental, etc.)

☐ Total rating (max 20p)	Child friendly ☐ Yes ☐ No	Dog friendly ☐ Yes ☐ No	For the disabled ☐ Yes ☐ No	Want to return ☐ Yes ☐ No

⊙ Capentum Förlag

Activities

Route taken	Beginning mileage
	Ending mileage
Rest area (Place name, town, distance, standard of sanitation and surroundings etc.)	Total miles traveled
	Total travel time
	Total fuel cost

We camped with / met

Excursions / Activities

The most positive / negative with this destination

To remember before the next visit

Destination

Location:		Campground ☐	Arrived – Departed – Year
Address:		Parking area ☐	First visit ☐ Return visit ☐
GPS:		Wild-camp ☐	Check in from / Check out until
Website:		Other ☐	Weather

Caravan ☐ Tent/Van ☐ Motorhome ☐ Cabin ☐	Site nr	Site price/day	Elec.price/day	Booked site ☐Yes ☐No	Price worthy ☐Yes ☐No

☐ **Environment (1-5)** (Location, surroundings, size of plot or cabin, maintenance, distance to electrical outlet etc.)

☐ **Sanitary (1-5)** (Standard of sanitation, room for cooking and washing, waterfilling, waste disposal etc.)

☐ **Service (1-5)** (Service from staff, info material, booking, shops, restaurants, wifi access etc.)

☐ **Activities (1-5)** (Playground, miniature golf, bath, fishing, hiking and running trails, boat/canoe/bicycle rental, etc.)

☐ Total rating (max 20p)	Child friendly ☐Yes ☐No	Dog friendly ☐Yes ☐No	For the disabled ☐Yes ☐No	Want to return ☐Yes ☐No

Activities

Route taken	Beginning mileage
	Ending mileage

Rest area (Place name, town, distance, standard of sanitation and surroundings etc.)	Total miles traveled
	Total travel time
	Total fuel cost

We camped with / met

Excursions / Activities

The most positive / negative with this destination

To remember before the next visit

Destination

Location:		Campground ☐	Arrived – Departed – Year

Address:		Parking area ☐	First visit ☐ Return visit ☐

GPS:		Wild-camp ☐	Check in from	Check out until

Website:		Other ☐	Weather

Caravan ☐ Tent/Van ☐ Motorhome ☐ Cabin ☐	Site nr	Site price/day	Elec.price/day	Booked site ☐Yes ☐No	Price worthy ☐Yes ☐No

☐ **Environment (1–5)** (Location, surroundings, size of plot or cabin, maintenance, distance to electrical outlet etc.)

☐ **Sanitary (1–5)** (Standard of sanitation, room for cooking and washing, waterfilling, waste disposal etc.)

☐ **Service (1–5)** (Service from staff, info material, booking, shops, restaurants, wifi access etc.)

☐ **Activities (1–5)** (Playground, miniature golf, bath, fishing, hiking and running trails, boat/canoe/bicycle rental, etc.)

☐ Total rating (max 20p)	Child friendly ☐Yes ☐No	Dog friendly ☐Yes ☐No	For the disabled ☐Yes ☐No	Want to return ☐Yes ☐No

● Capentum Förlag

Activities

Route taken	Beginning mileage
	Ending mileage
Rest area (Place name, town, distance, standard of sanitation and surroundings etc.)	Total miles traveled
	Total travel time
	Total fuel cost

We camped with / met

Excursions / Activities

The most positive / negative with this destination

To remember before the next visit

Destination

Location:	Campground ☐	Arrived – Departed – Year
Address:	Parking area ☐	First visit ☐ Return visit ☐
GPS:	Wild-camp ☐	Check in from — Check out until
Website:	Other ☐	Weather

Caravan ☐ Tent/Van ☐ Motorhome ☐ Cabin ☐	Site nr	Site price/day	Elec.price/day	Booked site ☐Yes ☐No	Price worthy ☐Yes ☐No

☐ Environment (1-5) (Location, surroundings, size of plot or cabin, maintenance, distance to electrical outlet etc.)

☐ Sanitary (1-5) (Standard of sanitation, room for cooking and washing, waterfilling, waste disposal etc.)

☐ Service (1-5) (Service from staff, info material, booking, shops, restaurants, wifi access etc.)

☐ Activities (1-5) (Playground, miniature golf, bath, fishing, hiking and running trails, boat/canoe/bicycle rental, etc.)

☐ Total rating (max 20p)	Child friendly ☐Yes ☐No	Dog friendly ☐Yes ☐No	For the disabled ☐Yes ☐No	Want to return ☐Yes ☐No

© Capentum Förlag

Activities

Route taken	Beginning mileage
	Ending mileage
Rest area (Place name, town, distance, standard of sanitation and surroundings etc.)	Total miles traveled
	Total travel time
	Total fuel cost

We camped with / met

Excursions / Activities

The most positive / negative with this destination

To remember before the next visit

Destination

Location:		Campground ☐	Arrived – Departed – Year
Address:		Parking area ☐	First visit ☐ Return visit ☐
GPS:		Wild-camp ☐	Check in from	Check out until
Website:		Other ☐	Weather

Caravan ☐ Tent/Van ☐ Motorhome ☐ Cabin ☐	Site nr	Site price/day	Elec.price/day	Booked site ☐ Yes ☐ No	Price worthy ☐ Yes ☐ No

☐ **Environment (1-5)** (Location, surroundings, size of plot or cabin, maintenance, distance to electrical outlet etc.)

☐ **Sanitary (1-5)** (Standard of sanitation, room for cooking and washing, waterfilling, waste disposal etc.)

☐ **Service (1-5)** (Service from staff, info material, booking, shops, restaurants, wifi access etc.)

☐ **Activities (1-5)** (Playground, miniature golf, bath, fishing, hiking and running trails, boat/canoe/bicycle rental, etc.)

☐ Total rating (max 20p)	Child friendly ☐ Yes ☐ No	Dog friendly ☐ Yes ☐ No	For the disabled ☐ Yes ☐ No	Want to return ☐ Yes ☐ No

© Capentum Förlag

Activities

Route taken		Beginning mileage
		Ending mileage
Rest area (Place name, town, distance, standard of sanitation and surroundings etc.)		Total miles traveled
		Total travel time
		Total fuel cost

We camped with / met

Excursions / Activities

The most positive / negative with this destination

To remember before the next visit

Destination

Location:	Campground ☐	Arrived – Departed – Year	
Address:	Parking area ☐	First visit ☐ Return visit ☐	
GPS:	Wild-camp ☐	Check in from	Check out until
Website:	Other ☐	Weather	

Caravan ☐ Tent/Van ☐ Motorhome ☐ Cabin ☐	Site nr	Site price/day	Elec.price/day	Booked site ☐Yes ☐No	Price worthy ☐Yes ☐No

☐ Environment (1-5) (Location, surroundings, size of plot or cabin, maintenance, distance to electrical outlet etc.)

☐ Sanitary (1-5) (Standard of sanitation, room for cooking and washing, waterfilling, waste disposal etc.)

☐ Service (1-5) (Service from staff, info material, booking, shops, restaurants, wifi access etc.)

☐ Activities (1-5) (Playground, miniature golf, bath, fishing, hiking and running trails, boat/canoe/bicycle rental, etc.)

☐ Total rating (max 20p)	Child friendly ☐Yes ☐No	Dog friendly ☐Yes ☐No	For the disabled ☐Yes ☐No	Want to return ☐Yes ☐No

Activities

Route taken	Beginning mileage
	Ending mileage
Rest area (Place name, town, distance, standard of sanitation and surroundings etc.)	Total miles traveled
	Total travel time
	Total fuel cost

We camped with / met

Excursions / Activities

The most positive / negative with this destination

To remember before the next visit

Destination

Location:		Campground ☐	Arrived – Departed – Year	
Address:		Parking area ☐	First visit ☐ Return visit ☐	
GPS:		Wild-camp ☐	Check in from	Check out until
Website:		Other ☐	Weather	

Caravan ☐ Motorhome ☐	Tent/Van ☐ Cabin ☐	Site nr	Site price/day	Elec.price/day	Booked site ☐ Yes ☐ No	Price worthy ☐ Yes ☐ No

☐ **Environment (1–5)** (Location, surroundings, size of plot or cabin, maintenance, distance to electrical outlet etc.)

☐ **Sanitary (1–5)** (Standard of sanitation, room for cooking and washing, waterfilling, waste disposal etc.)

☐ **Service (1–5)** (Service from staff, info material, booking, shops, restaurants, wifi access etc.)

☐ **Activities (1–5)** (Playground, miniature golf, bath, fishing, hiking and running trails, boat/canoe/bicycle rental, etc.)

☐ Total rating (max 20p)	Child friendly ☐ Yes ☐ No	Dog friendly ☐ Yes ☐ No	For the disabled ☐ Yes ☐ No	Want to return ☐ Yes ☐ No

© Capentum Förlag

Activities

Route taken	Beginning mileage
	Ending mileage
Rest area (Place name, town, distance, standard of sanitation and surroundings etc.)	Total miles traveled
	Total travel time
	Total fuel cost

We camped with / met

Excursions / Activities

The most positive / negative with this destination

To remember before the next visit

Destination

Location:	Campground ☐	Arrived – Departed – Year
Address:	Parking area ☐	First visit ☐ / Return visit ☐
GPS:	Wild-camp ☐	Check in from / Check out until
Website:	Other ☐	Weather

Caravan ☐ Tent/Van ☐	Site nr	Site price/day	Elec.price/day	Booked site	Price worthy
Motorhome ☐ Cabin ☐				☐ Yes ☐ No	☐ Yes ☐ No

☐ **Environment (1-5)** (Location, surroundings, size of plot or cabin, maintenance, distance to electrical outlet etc.)

☐ **Sanitary (1-5)** (Standard of sanitation, room for cooking and washing, waterfilling, waste disposal etc.)

☐ **Service (1-5)** (Service from staff, info material, booking, shops, restaurants, wifi access etc.)

☐ **Activities (1-5)** (Playground, miniature golf, bath, fishing, hiking and running trails, boat/canoe/bicycle rental, etc.)

☐ Total rating (max 20p)	Child friendly ☐ Yes ☐ No	Dog friendly ☐ Yes ☐ No	For the disabled ☐ Yes ☐ No	Want to return ☐ Yes ☐ No

Activities

Route taken	Beginning mileage
	Ending mileage
Rest area (Place name, town, distance, standard of sanitation and surroundings etc.)	Total miles traveled
	Total travel time
	Total fuel cost

We camped with / met

Excursions / Activities

The most positive / negative with this destination

To remember before the next visit

Destination

Location:		Campground ☐	Arrived – Departed – Year
Address:		Parking area ☐	First visit ☐ Return visit ☐
GPS:		Wild-camp ☐	Check in from / Check out until
Website:		Other ☐	Weather

Caravan ☐ Tent/Van ☐ Motorhome ☐ Cabin ☐	Site nr	Site price/day	Elec.price/day	Booked site ☐ Yes ☐ No	Price worthy ☐ Yes ☐ No

☐ **Environment (1–5)** (Location, surroundings, size of plot or cabin, maintenance, distance to electrical outlet etc.)

☐ **Sanitary (1–5)** (Standard of sanitation, room for cooking and washing, waterfilling, waste disposal etc.)

☐ **Service (1–5)** (Service from staff, info material, booking, shops, restaurants, wifi access etc.)

☐ **Activities (1–5)** (Playground, miniature golf, bath, fishing, hiking and running trails, boat/canoe/bicycle rental, etc.)

☐ Total rating (max 20p)	Child friendly ☐ Yes ☐ No	Dog friendly ☐ Yes ☐ No	For the disabled ☐ Yes ☐ No	Want to return ☐ Yes ☐ No

⊙ Capentum Förlag

Activities

Route taken	Beginning mileage
	Ending mileage
Rest area (Place name, town, distance, standard of sanitation and surroundings etc.)	Total miles traveled
	Total travel time
	Total fuel cost

We camped with / met

Excursions / Activities

The most positive / negative with this destination

To remember before the next visit

Destination

Location:		Campground ☐	Arrived – Departed – Year
Address:		Parking area ☐	First visit ☐ Return visit ☐
GPS:		Wild-camp ☐	Check in from / Check out until
Website:		Other ☐	Weather

Caravan ☐ Tent/Van ☐ Motorhome ☐ Cabin ☐	Site nr	Site price/day	Elec.price/day	Booked site ☐ Yes ☐ No	Price worthy ☐ Yes ☐ No

☐ **Environment (1-5)** (Location, surroundings, size of plot or cabin, maintenance, distance to electrical outlet etc.)

☐ **Sanitary (1-5)** (Standard of sanitation, room for cooking and washing, waterfilling, waste disposal etc.)

☐ **Service (1-5)** (Service from staff, info material, booking, shops, restaurants, wifi access etc.)

☐ **Activities (1-5)** (Playground, miniature golf, bath, fishing, hiking and running trails, boat/canoe/bicycle rental, etc.)

☐ Total rating (max 20p)	Child friendly ☐ Yes ☐ No	Dog friendly ☐ Yes ☐ No	For the disabled ☐ Yes ☐ No	Want to return ☐ Yes ☐ No

Activities

Route taken		Beginning mileage
		Ending mileage
Rest area (Place name, town, distance, standard of sanitation and surroundings etc.)		Total miles traveled
		Total travel time
		Total fuel cost

We camped with / met

Excursions / Activities

The most positive / negative with this destination

To remember before the next visit

Destination

Location:	Campground ☐	Arrived – Departed – Year
Address:	Parking area ☐	First visit ☐ Return visit ☐
GPS:	Wild-camp ☐	Check in from / Check out until
Website:	Other ☐	Weather

Caravan ☐ Tent/Van ☐ Motorhome ☐ Cabin ☐	Site nr	Site price/day	Elec.price/day	Booked site ☐ Yes ☐ No	Price worthy ☐ Yes ☐ No

☐ **Environment (1-5)** (Location, surroundings, size of plot or cabin, maintenance, distance to electrical outlet etc.)

☐ **Sanitary (1-5)** (Standard of sanitation, room for cooking and washing, waterfilling, waste disposal etc.)

☐ **Service (1-5)** (Service from staff, info material, booking, shops, restaurants, wifi access etc.)

☐ **Activities (1-5)** (Playground, miniature golf, bath, fishing, hiking and running trails, boat/canoe/bicycle rental, etc.)

☐ Total rating (max 20p)	Child friendly ☐ Yes ☐ No	Dog friendly ☐ Yes ☐ No	For the disabled ☐ Yes ☐ No	Want to return ☐ Yes ☐ No

● Capentum Förlag

Activities

Route taken		Beginning mileage
		Ending mileage
Rest area (Place name, town, distance, standard of sanitation and surroundings etc.)		Total miles traveled
		Total travel time
		Total fuel cost

We camped with / met

Excursions / Activities

The most positive / negative with this destination

To remember before the next visit

Destination

Location:		Campground ☐	Arrived – Departed – Year
Address:		Parking area ☐	First visit ☐ Return visit ☐
GPS:		Wild-camp ☐	Check in from / Check out until
Website:		Other ☐	Weather

Caravan ☐ Tent/Van ☐ Motorhome ☐ Cabin ☐	Site nr	Site price/day	Elec.price/day	Booked site ☐ Yes ☐ No	Price worthy ☐ Yes ☐ No

☐ **Environment (1-5)** (Location, surroundings, size of plot or cabin, maintenance, distance to electrical outlet etc.)

☐ **Sanitary (1-5)** (Standard of sanitation, room for cooking and washing, waterfilling, waste disposal etc.)

☐ **Service (1-5)** (Service from staff, info material, booking, shops, restaurants, wifi access etc.)

☐ **Activities (1-5)** (Playground, miniature golf, bath, fishing, hiking and running trails, boat/canoe/bicycle rental, etc.)

☐ Total rating (max 20p)	Child friendly ☐ Yes ☐ No	Dog friendly ☐ Yes ☐ No	For the disabled ☐ Yes ☐ No	Want to return ☐ Yes ☐ No

© Capentum Förlag

Activities

Route taken		Beginning mileage
		Ending mileage
Rest area (Place name, town, distance, standard of sanitation and surroundings etc.)		Total miles traveled
		Total travel time
		Total fuel cost

We camped with / met

Excursions / Activities

The most positive / negative with this destination

To remember before the next visit

Destination

Location:	Campground ☐	Arrived – Departed – Year	
Address:	Parking area ☐	First visit ☐ Return visit ☐	
GPS:	Wild-camp ☐	Check in from	Check out until
Website:	Other ☐	Weather	

Caravan ☐ Tent/Van ☐ Motorhome ☐ Cabin ☐	Site nr	Site price/day	Elec.price/day	Booked site ☐ Yes ☐ No	Price worthy ☐ Yes ☐ No

☐ Environment (1-5) (Location, surroundings, size of plot or cabin, maintenance, distance to electrical outlet etc.)

☐ Sanitary (1-5) (Standard of sanitation, room for cooking and washing, waterfilling, waste disposal etc.)

☐ Service (1-5) (Service from staff, info material, booking, shops, restaurants, wifi access etc.)

☐ Activities (1-5) (Playground, miniature golf, bath, fishing, hiking and running trails, boat/canoe/bicycle rental, etc.)

☐ Total rating (max 20p)	Child friendly ☐ Yes ☐ No	Dog friendly ☐ Yes ☐ No	For the disabled ☐ Yes ☐ No	Want to return ☐ Yes ☐ No

Capentum Förlag

Activities

Route taken		Beginning mileage
		Ending mileage
Rest area (Place name, town, distance, standard of sanitation and surroundings etc.)		Total miles traveled
		Total travel time
		Total fuel cost

We camped with / met

Excursions / Activities

The most positive / negative with this destination

To remember before the next visit

Destination

Location:		Campground ☐	Arrived – Departed – Year

Address:		Parking area ☐	First visit ☐ Return visit ☐

GPS:		Wild-camp ☐	Check in from	Check out until

Website:		Other ☐	Weather

Caravan ☐ Tent/Van ☐ Motorhome ☐ Cabin ☐	Site nr	Site price/day	Elec.price/day	Booked site ☐ Yes ☐ No	Price worthy ☐ Yes ☐ No

☐ **Environment (1-5)** (Location, surroundings, size of plot or cabin, maintenance, distance to electrical outlet etc.)

☐ **Sanitary (1-5)** (Standard of sanitation, room for cooking and washing, waterfilling, waste disposal etc.)

☐ **Service (1-5)** (Service from staff, info material, booking, shops, restaurants, wifi access etc.)

☐ **Activities (1-5)** (Playground, miniature golf, bath, fishing, hiking and running trails, boat/canoe/bicycle rental, etc.)

☐ Total rating (max 20p)	Child friendly ☐ Yes ☐ No	Dog friendly ☐ Yes ☐ No	For the disabled ☐ Yes ☐ No	Want to return ☐ Yes ☐ No

© Capentum Förlag

Activities

Route taken	Beginning mileage
	Ending mileage
Rest area (Place name, town, distance, standard of sanitation and surroundings etc.)	Total miles traveled
	Total travel time
	Total fuel cost

We camped with / met

Excursions / Activities

The most positive / negative with this destination

To remember before the next visit

Destination

Location:	Campground ☐	Arrived – Departed – Year
Address:	Parking area ☐	First visit ☐ Return visit ☐
GPS:	Wild-camp ☐	Check in from	Check out until
Website:	Other ☐	Weather

Caravan ☐ Tent/Van ☐ Motorhome ☐ Cabin ☐	Site nr	Site price/day	Elec.price/day	Booked site ☐ Yes ☐ No	Price worthy ☐ Yes ☐ No

☐ **Environment (1-5)** (Location, surroundings, size of plot or cabin, maintenance, distance to electrical outlet etc.)

☐ **Sanitary (1-5)** (Standard of sanitation, room for cooking and washing, waterfilling, waste disposal etc.)

☐ **Service (1-5)** (Service from staff, info material, booking, shops, restaurants, wifi access etc.)

☐ **Activities (1-5)** (Playground, miniature golf, bath, fishing, hiking and running trails, boat/canoe/bicycle rental, etc.)

☐ Total rating (max 20p)	Child friendly ☐ Yes ☐ No	Dog friendly ☐ Yes ☐ No	For the disabled ☐ Yes ☐ No	Want to return ☐ Yes ☐ No

© Capentum Förlag

Activities

Route taken	Beginning mileage
	Ending mileage
Rest area (Place name, town, distance, standard of sanitation and surroundings etc.)	Total miles traveled
	Total travel time
	Total fuel cost

We camped with / met

Excursions / Activities

The most positive / negative with this destination

To remember before the next visit

Destination

Location:		Campground ☐	Arrived – Departed – Year
Address:		Parking area ☐	First visit ☐ Return visit ☐
GPS:		Wild-camp ☐	Check in from / Check out until
Website:		Other ☐	Weather

Caravan ☐ Motorhome ☐	Tent/Van ☐ Cabin ☐	Site nr	Site price/day	Elec.price/day	Booked site ☐ Yes ☐ No	Price worthy ☐ Yes ☐ No

☐ **Environment (1-5)** (Location, surroundings, size of plot or cabin, maintenance, distance to electrical outlet etc.)

☐ **Sanitary (1-5)** (Standard of sanitation, room for cooking and washing, waterfilling, waste disposal etc.)

☐ **Service (1-5)** (Service from staff, info material, booking, shops, restaurants, wifi access etc.)

☐ **Activities (1-5)** (Playground, miniature golf, bath, fishing, hiking and running trails, boat/canoe/bicycle rental, etc.)

☐ Total rating (max 20p)	Child friendly ☐ Yes ☐ No	Dog friendly ☐ Yes ☐ No	For the disabled ☐ Yes ☐ No	Want to return ☐ Yes ☐ No

Activities

Route taken	Beginning mileage
	Ending mileage

Rest area (Place name, town, distance, standard of sanitation and surroundings etc.)	Total miles traveled
	Total travel time
	Total fuel cost

We camped with / met

Excursions / Activities

The most positive / negative with this destination

To remember before the next visit

Destination

Location:	Campground ☐	Arrived – Departed – Year
Address:	Parking area ☐	First visit ☐ Return visit ☐
GPS:	Wild-camp ☐	Check in from / Check out until
Website:	Other ☐	Weather

Caravan ☐ Tent/Van ☐ Motorhome ☐ Cabin ☐	Site nr	Site price/day	Elec.price/day	Booked site ☐ Yes ☐ No	Price worthy ☐ Yes ☐ No

☐ **Environment (1–5)** (Location, surroundings, size of plot or cabin, maintenance, distance to electrical outlet etc.)

☐ **Sanitary (1–5)** (Standard of sanitation, room for cooking and washing, waterfilling, waste disposal etc.)

☐ **Service (1–5)** (Service from staff, info material, booking, shops, restaurants, wifi access etc.)

☐ **Activities (1–5)** (Playground, miniature golf, bath, fishing, hiking and running trails, boat/canoe/bicycle rental, etc.)

☐ Total rating (max 20p)	Child friendly ☐ Yes ☐ No	Dog friendly ☐ Yes ☐ No	For the disabled ☐ Yes ☐ No	Want to return ☐ Yes ☐ No

© Capentum Förlag

Activities

Route taken		Beginning mileage
		Ending mileage
Rest area (Place name, town, distance, standard of sanitation and surroundings etc.)		Total miles traveled
		Total travel time
		Total fuel cost

We camped with / met

Excursions / Activities

The most positive / negative with this destination

To remember before the next visit

Destination

Location:		Campground ☐	Arrived – Departed – Year
Address:		Parking area ☐	First visit ☐ Return visit ☐
GPS:		Wild-camp ☐	Check in from / Check out until
Website:		Other ☐	Weather

Caravan ☐ Tent/Van ☐ Motorhome ☐ Cabin ☐	Site nr	Site price/day	Elec.price/day	Booked site ☐ Yes ☐ No	Price worthy ☐ Yes ☐ No

☐ **Environment (1-5)** (Location, surroundings, size of plot or cabin, maintenance, distance to electrical outlet etc.)

☐ **Sanitary (1-5)** (Standard of sanitation, room for cooking and washing, waterfilling, waste disposal etc.)

☐ **Service (1-5)** (Service from staff, info material, booking, shops, restaurants, wifi access etc.)

☐ **Activities (1-5)** (Playground, miniature golf, bath, fishing, hiking and running trails, boat/canoe/bicycle rental, etc.)

☐ Total rating (max 20p)	Child friendly ☐ Yes ☐ No	Dog friendly ☐ Yes ☐ No	For the disabled ☐ Yes ☐ No	Want to return ☐ Yes ☐ No

Activities

Route taken		Beginning mileage
		Ending mileage
Rest area (Place name, town, distance, standard of sanitation and surroundings etc.)		Total miles traveled
		Total travel time
		Total fuel cost

We camped with / met

Excursions / Activities

The most positive / negative with this destination

To remember before the next visit

Destination

Location:		Campground ☐	Arrived – Departed – Year
Address:		Parking area ☐	First visit ☐ Return visit ☐
GPS:		Wild–camp ☐	Check in from / Check out until
Website:		Other ☐	Weather

Caravan ☐ Tent/Van ☐ Motorhome ☐ Cabin ☐	Site nr	Site price/day	Elec.price/day	Booked site ☐ Yes ☐ No	Price worthy ☐ Yes ☐ No

☐ **Environment (1-5)** (Location, surroundings, size of plot or cabin, maintenance, distance to electrical outlet etc.)

☐ **Sanitary (1-5)** (Standard of sanitation, room for cooking and washing, waterfilling, waste disposal etc.)

☐ **Service (1-5)** (Service from staff, info material, booking, shops, restaurants, wifi access etc.)

☐ **Activities (1-5)** (Playground, miniature golf, bath, fishing, hiking and running trails, boat/canoe/bicycle rental, etc.)

☐ Total rating (max 20p)	Child friendly ☐ Yes ☐ No	Dog friendly ☐ Yes ☐ No	For the disabled ☐ Yes ☐ No	Want to return ☐ Yes ☐ No

⊙ Capentum Förlag

Activities

Route taken	Beginning mileage
	Ending mileage
Rest area (Place name, town, distance, standard of sanitation and surroundings etc.)	Total miles traveled
	Total travel time
	Total fuel cost

We camped with / met

Excursions / Activities

The most positive / negative with this destination

To remember before the next visit